Fact Finders™

Biographies

Cesar Chavez

Champion of Workers

by Tyler Schumacher

Consultant:
Clete Daniel, Professor of American Labor History
School of Industrial and Labor Relations
Cornell University
Ithaca, New York

Capstone
press

Mankato, Minnesota

jB
CHAVEZ

JY BB

Fact Finders is published by Capstone Press,
151 Good Counsel Drive, P.O. Box 669, Mankato, Minnesota 56002.
www.capstonepress.com

Library of Congress Cataloging-in-Publication Data
Schumacher, Tyler.
    Cesar Chavez : champion of workers / by Tyler Schumacher.
    p. cm.—(Fact finders. Biographies. Great Hispanics)
    Summary: "A brief introduction to the life of Cesar Chavez, the Mexican American
activist who founded the first successful farm workers' union in the United States"
—Provided by publisher.
    Includes bibliographical references and index.
    ISBN-13: 978-0-7368-5436-8 (hardcover)
    ISBN-10: 0-7368-5436-3 (hardcover)
    1. Chavez, Cesar, 1927—Juvenile literature. 2. Labor leaders—United
states—Biography—Juvenile literature. 3. Mexican American migrant agricultural
laborers—Biography—Juvenile literature. I. Title. II. Series.
HD6509.C48S38 2006
331.88′13′092—dc22   2005015594

Editorial Credits
Jennifer Besel, editor; Juliette Peters, set designer; Linda Clavel, book designer;
    Wanda Winch, photo researcher/photo editor

Photo Credits
AP/Associated Press, 21; Corbis/Bettmann, 19, 22; Corbis/Hulton-Deutsch Collection,
cover; Corbis/Najlah Feanny, 27; Getty Images Inc./Time Life Pictures/Arthur Schatz, 1,
17; Jocelyn Sherman, 25; Oakland Museum of California/Dorothea Lange Collection, Gift
of Paul S. Taylor, 11; Photo Courtesy of the Cesar E. Chavez Foundation, 7; Take Stock/
George Ballis, 18; Texas A&M University-Corpus Christi/Bell Library/Special Collections
and Archives, E.E. Mireles & Jovita G. Mireles, 8; Wayne State University/Walter P. Reuther
Library, 4–5, 9, 12, 13, 14–15, 16, 23, 26

1 2 3 4 5 6 11 10 09 08 07 06

Table of Contents

Chapter 1

Birth of a Union

Cesar Chavez looked out at the crowded theater in Fresno, California. More than 100 **migrant workers** stared back at him. Most of them were Mexican. Farm owners hired these people to work in their fields, but they paid them very low **wages**. The workers had poor housing and almost nothing to eat. Chavez believed if they joined together they could make owners improve these conditions. He had gathered the workers in Fresno to start a **union**.

The First Step

Chavez called his union the National Farm Workers Association (NFWA). He believed the union could be especially helpful to people who spoke Spanish.

Chavez, far right, and the other organizers of the union stood in front of the National Farm Workers Association's flag.

Chavez told the group a union could make farm owners pay fair wages. The farmworkers agreed. They voted to make Chavez the union's president.

That day, Chavez's dream of a farmworkers' union became real. He would spend the rest of his life as a champion of workers' rights.

Chapter 2

Childhood

Cesario Estrada Chavez was born March 31, 1927, into a loving and hardworking family. As the second of six children, Chavez was very close to his family. He helped in the family's grocery store and on their farm in Yuma, Arizona.

Chavez's parents were patient and understanding. His mother, Juana, taught him to be kind to all people. She also taught him never to use violence. His father, Librado, taught him all about animals and farming.

Chavez had a Mexican heritage. His grandfather had come to the United States from Mexico to start a better life. Chavez's mother was also born in Mexico. The Chavez family spoke Spanish at home.

As a child, Chavez spent much of his time with family and friends on the family farm.

School and Work

Chavez's early life was divided between school and farmwork. Early each morning, he fed the family's animals and gathered eggs.

When his chores were finished, he went to school. Chavez did not like school. Teachers punished him for speaking Spanish. They didn't respect his Mexican heritage.

Mexican students in the United States were not allowed to speak Spanish. ▼

▲ A few walls of the Chavez family home in Arizona are still standing.

Losing the Farm

The Great Depression (1929–1939) spread through the United States during the 1930s. Businesses closed and many people lost their jobs. Chavez's family had to sell their store and farm. In 1938, the family moved to California to find work.

Chapter 3

Farmworkers

In California, Chavez's family moved from town to town looking for work. Chavez learned that life as a migrant worker was not easy. Most fields had no bathrooms or drinking water. Owners paid workers barely enough money to buy food. One-room shacks or tents were the only homes they could afford. But the workers had no choice but to live in these poor conditions. Owners would not listen to them or help them.

Hard Work

Chavez's family picked crops, such as lettuce and sugar beets. They spent whole days bent over in the fields. Their backs hurt.

Migrant workers often lived in run-down communities called barrios.

▲ Migrant workers bent over all day, picking crops. Many had back pain their whole lives.

The Chavez children worked in the fields with their parents. After eighth grade, Chavez quit school to work in the fields full-time. He was never able to attend high school.

Librado's Lesson

There were no laws to protect farmworkers' pay. Owners could lower wages if they wanted. Chavez's father, Librado, wouldn't work for owners who cheated people out of money. If an owner began cheating workers, Librado stopped picking. He would **strike** with other workers. Librado taught Chavez to stand up for what he believed in.

Helen Fabela

As a teenager, Chavez met a young girl named Helen Fabela. Fabela was also from a family of farmworkers. She had quit school to make money for her family. Chavez visited Fabela at the grocery store where she worked. In 1948, the two were married. Over the next 10 years, they had eight children.

Chavez and his wife had both worked in the fields. They knew how hard life was for farmworkers. The couple wanted to help. Together they taught many farmworkers to read and write. They also helped many people from Mexico become U.S. citizens.

After their wedding, the Chavezes took a vacation along the California coast. ▼

Chapter 4

Serving the People

In 1952, Chavez took a job with the Community Service Organization (CSO) in San Jose, California. The CSO taught Mexican Americans about their rights. While working for the CSO, Chavez learned how to organize people. He learned ways to form groups and how to run events. He found he was very good at leading people.

Starting a Union

Chavez knew conditions for farmworkers were not getting any better. Thousands of migrant workers were looking for jobs in California.

With the CSO, Chavez (far right) worked hard to get Mexican Americans to vote in elections.

Some migrants were willing to work for any pay, even very low wages. Farm owners took advantage of these workers. Workers picked crops all day for only a few dollars.

Chavez's wife and children moved to Delano with him to help start the union.

Chavez believed farm owners were unfair to workers. He felt workers needed to form a union to protect their rights. He believed a union could change farmworkers' lives. Chavez decided to quit his job at the CSO to form a union.

Chavez wanted to form a union that would make owners change their ways. But he needed to find a place to start. Many workers picked grapes in Delano, California. Farm owners there paid workers some of the lowest wages in California. Chavez decided to move his family and start the union in Delano.

Chavez and a small group of helpers worked hard to start the union. Some workers were scared that owners would not hire them if they joined. Chavez told them a union could make owners treat them better. Because Chavez had worked in the fields, workers believed he understood their problems. Many workers joined Chavez. In 1962, they started the National Farm Workers Association (NFWA).

▲ Chavez had to answer a lot of questions from farmworkers to convince them to form a union.

The Grape Strike

In 1965, grape farm owners in Delano lowered workers' wages. The NFWA stood up to the owners by going on strike. Union members refused to work until owners gave them better wages and working conditions.

F A C T !

Chavez believed anything was possible with hard work. His favorite saying was *"Si se puede,"* which means "Yes, it can be done."

Chavez marched in picket lines with other union members during the grape strike. ▼

The owners would not listen. Chavez decided to ask the government for help. With about 100 union members, he marched 300 miles (483 kilometers) to Sacramento.

Although the governor did not respond, the march was a success. It brought the workers' needs to the public's attention. The union used this attention to ask Americans to **boycott** grapes. The boycott caused many owners to lose money.

A Nonviolent Fight

Farm owners were not happy that their grapes weren't being picked or sold. But instead of talking with the union, owners got angry. Some owners hired people to attack union members.

18

Chavez believed arguments should be settled without violence. To remind the union to stay peaceful, Chavez started a fast.

Chavez did not eat for 25 days. He became very weak. Other members had to work together to keep the union going. Chavez's fast succeeded in bringing peace to the union.

Victory for Workers

After five long years, the grape strike ended. The boycott had hurt the owners. To stop the boycott, several owners agreed to improve wages and working conditions.

Victory did not come without cost. During the strike, workers didn't earn wages. Chavez said about 95 percent of the workers lost their homes and cars.

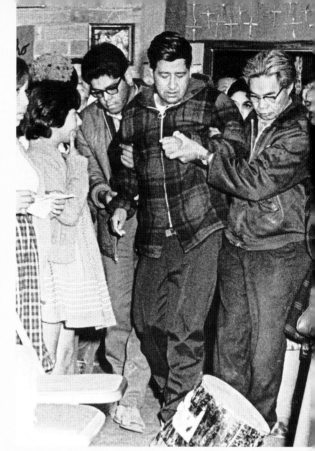

▲ Chavez was very weak during his fast. He needed help walking even short distances.

QUOTE

"Because we have suffered, and we are not afraid to suffer in order to survive, we are ready to give up everything—even our lives—in our struggle for justice."
—Cesar Chavez

Chapter 5

More Work to Do

During the five-year grape strike, the NFWA went through some changes. In 1966, a union called the Agricultural Workers Organizing Committee (AWOC) was trying to help Filipino farmworkers. The AWOC had gone on strike in Delano too. In order to help all migrant workers, the two unions joined together. They became known as the United Farm Workers (UFW). Chavez was chosen to lead the new union.

In the 1970s, with the UFW behind him, Chavez again asked California's government for help. In 1975, he got it. The legislature passed the Agricultural Labor Relations Act, guaranteeing farmworkers the right to organize into unions.

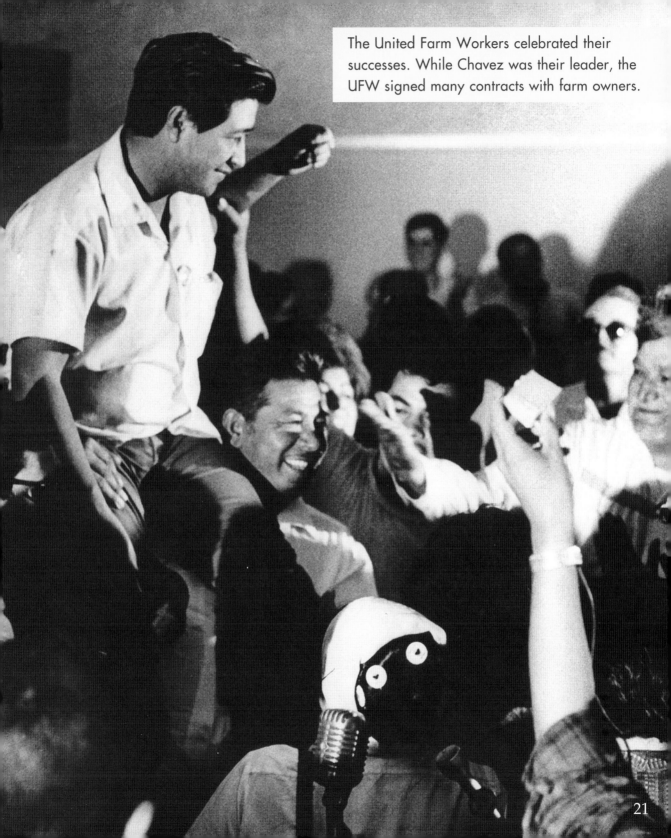

The United Farm Workers celebrated their successes. While Chavez was their leader, the UFW signed many contracts with farm owners.

Pesticides

During the 1980s, Chavez tried to change the use of **pesticides** on crops. These chemicals could make farmworkers sick. In 1988, he fasted for 36 days to protest the use of pesticides. Many people asked the government to make pesticides against the law. The government made harmful pesticides illegal.

Chavez asked Americans to boycott grapes again in the 1980s to fight the use of pesticides. ⬇

Chavez on the Job

Chavez did have some problems of his own. Sometimes he would argue with people. Some people complained he was too bossy.

Chavez's job wasn't easy. He didn't make much money and he was often away from his family. Years of farmwork made his back hurt. But he never stopped helping workers.

⬆ The union wasn't always successful. Sometimes Chavez got frustrated.

Chapter 6

Champion of Workers

Chavez led his union for more than 30 years. He helped make life better for thousands of farmworkers, but he never used violence to reach his goals.

Even after he turned 60, Chavez continued to work. But his body slowly began to tire. During the night of April 23, 1993, Chavez died in his sleep. He was 66 years old.

A Real Hero

Thousands of people came to Chavez's funeral. They marched in the hot California sun to pay their respects.

Later, even Chavez's grandchildren marched to support farmworkers.

Leaders from around the world sent messages. President Bill Clinton called Chavez a real hero.

"Cesar Chavez left our world better than he found it, and his legacy inspires us still."

—From the Presidential Medal of Freedom presentation

In 1994, Helen Chavez accepted the Presidential Medal of Freedom for her late husband. ⬇

Living On

In 1994, President Clinton honored Chavez with the Presidential Medal of Freedom. This award is the country's highest honor for good **citizenship**. Chavez was the second Mexican American to be given this honor.

People continue to remember and honor Cesar Chavez. Many cities have schools, parks, and libraries named after him. His face is on a U.S. postage stamp. But most important, the union he led continues to help farmworkers have better lives.

Fast Facts

Full name: Cesario Estrada Chavez

Birth: March 31, 1927

Death: April 23, 1993

Parents: Librado and Juana Chavez

Siblings: three sisters, two brothers

Wife: Helen Fabela Chavez

Daughters: Sylvia, Linda, Eloise, Anna, Elizabeth

Sons: Fernando, Paul, Anthony

Hometown: Yuma, Arizona

Achievements:

- Established the National Farm Workers Association in 1962
- Received the Presidential Medal of Freedom in 1994

Time Line

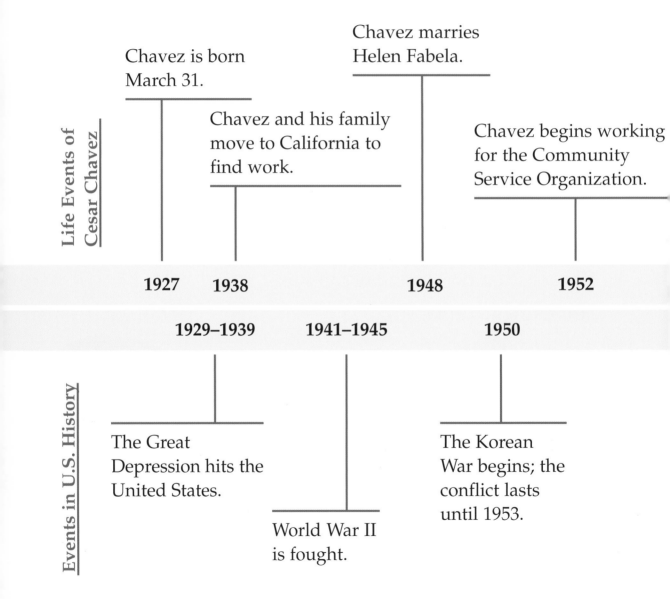

Life Events of Cesar Chavez

Chavez is born March 31.

Chavez and his family move to California to find work.

Chavez marries Helen Fabela.

Chavez begins working for the Community Service Organization.

1927   1938   1948   1952

1929–1939   1941–1945   1950

Events in U.S. History

The Great Depression hits the United States.

World War II is fought.

The Korean War begins; the conflict lasts until 1953.

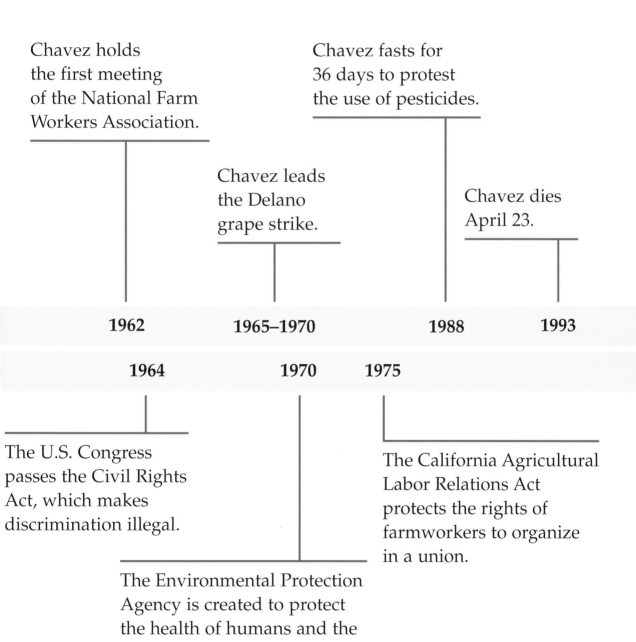

Chavez holds the first meeting of the National Farm Workers Association.

Chavez fasts for 36 days to protest the use of pesticides.

Chavez leads the Delano grape strike.

Chavez dies April 23.

1962   **1965–1970**   **1988**   **1993**

1964   **1970**   **1975**

The U.S. Congress passes the Civil Rights Act, which makes discrimination illegal.

The California Agricultural Labor Relations Act protects the rights of farmworkers to organize in a union.

The Environmental Protection Agency is created to protect the health of humans and the natural environment.

Glossary

boycott (BOI-kot)—to refuse to buy something as way of making a protest

citizenship (SIT-uh-zuhn-ship)—the quality of a person's actions in his or her community or country

migrant worker (MYE-gruhnt WURK-ur)—a farmworker who moves from place to place

pesticide (PESS-tuh-side)—a chemical used to kill pests such as insects

strike (STRIKE)—to refuse, as a group, to work because of a disagreement with an employer

union (YOON-yuhn)—an organized group of workers set up to improve working conditions and wages

wage (WAJE)—the money someone is paid for his or her work

Internet Sites

FactHound offers a safe, fun way to find Internet sites related to this book. All of the sites on FactHound have been researched by our staff.

Here's how:

1. Visit *www.facthound.com*
2. Type in this special code: **0736854363** for age-appropriate sites. Or enter a search word related to this book for a more general search.
3. Click on the **Fetch It** button.

FactHound will fetch the best sites for you!

Read More

Braun, Eric. *Cesar Chavez: Fighting for Farmworkers.* Graphic Library. Mankato, Minn.: Capstone Press, 2006.

Feinstein, Stephen. *Read about Cesar Chavez.* I Like Biographies! Berkeley Heights, N.J.: Enslow, 2004.

McLeese, Don. *Cesar E. Chavez.* Equal Rights Leaders. Vero Beach, Fla.: Rourke, 2003.

Index

Agricultural Workers
   Organizing Committee
   (AWOC), 20

California Agricultural
   Labor Relations Act, 20
Chavez, Cesar
   awards given to, 26, 27
   birth of, 6, 27
   childhood of, 6, 7, 8–9,
      10, 12
   children of, 13, 16, 27
   death of, 24, 27
   education of, 8, 12
   fasting of, 19, 22
Chavez, Helen Fabela
   (wife), 13, 16, 26, 27
Chavez, Juana (mother),
   6, 27
Chavez, Librado (father), 6,
   12, 27

Clinton, President Bill,
   25, 26
Community Service
   Organization (CSO),
   14–15, 16

Delano, California, 16, 17, 20
   grape boycott, 18–19
   grape strike, 17–19, 20

Great Depression, 9

National Farm Workers
   Association (NFWA),
   4–5, 17, 20, 27

pesticides, 22

United Farm Workers
   (UFW), 20, 21, 23, 24, 26